The

FAVOR of GOD

is REAL!

My Personal Testimonies

by Fola Sunny-Adeniyi

The Favor of God is Real!

My Personal Testimonies

Copyright ©2023 by Fola Sunny-Adeniyi

Published by **Joy Overflow Publications**

Editing by YourStoryYourLegacy – Ruth Yesmaniski

Layout by YourStoryYourLegacy – Ruth Yesmaniski

Cover Design by Jeshurun Writers

All rights reserved ©2023 Fola Sunny-Adeniyi

Unless otherwise noted, all Scripture quotations are taken from the Amplified® Bible, Copyright © 1954, 1958, 1962, 1964, 1965, 1987 by The Lockman Foundation. Used by permission.

Scripture quotations marked "TPT" are from The Passion Translation®. Copyright © 2017, 2018 by Passion & Fire Ministries, Inc. Used by permission. All rights reserved.

Printed in the U.S.A.

ISBN 978-1-7750128-3-2

PREFACE

My birth was mysterious and at the same time miraculous.

This is the story of my birth as told by my mother...My mum was happily married to my dad who is late now. They had it all good at the beginning of their marriage, but for unknown reasons, my dad started having affairs with strange women so the peace in their marriage was disrupted. My mother was heavily pregnant with me and was almost due for delivery. During one night, she was sound asleep when a force woke her up and instructed her to go and drown herself in the ocean. At that time they lived on Victoria Island, precisely Legico Flats, as it was known back then. It was very close to Bar Beach, a very popular beach in Lagos, Nigeria. When this voice told her to go drown herself in the ocean, she got up around 2 a.m. and began walking towards Bar Beach, completely in a trance like state. She explained that she knew it was not what she wanted to do, but the voice was louder and the force holding and pulling her was stronger than she could resist. As she was walking towards the beach, she noticed a car coming towards her; it was the only car on the road. When it reached the place she was at, the car stopped and a woman dressed in white regalia, stepped out and asked her, "Woman where are you going at this time of the night?"

She answered the woman of God, "I don't know, but a voice told me to go and drown myself in the ocean."

This baffled the woman of God.

That woman of God turned out to be the first female Christian leader to plant a church in Nigeria in 1925. Her name was Captain Christianah Abiodun Emanuel; the founder of Cherubim and Seraphim Church, with locations all over the world now. She was a very prophetic woman and was returning with her team from a night vigil when they saw my mum.

She picked my mum up in her car and took her to her home. On getting there, she instructed my mum to sleep on her bed for the night. After lying down for a while, my mum went into labor right there on the woman's bed and gave birth to me. I was born on July 16th, 1970.

In addition to being born on her bed, the woman also prophesied over my life. I am convinced the devil was trying to stop my birth by directing my mother to go drown herself. I am grateful to God that I am alive today to declare the goodness of the Lord in the land of the living.

"Before I formed you in the womb I knew [and] approved of you [as My chosen instrument], and before you were born I separated and set you apart, consecrating you; [and] I appointed you as a prophet to the nations. Jeremiah 1:5

This book is my testimony of how God has allowed signs, wonders and miracles to manifest in my life and lives of loved ones around me.

****

For well over 20 years now, the Lord had been impressing the numbers 4 and 19 to me, (not 419), but 4 and 19. I would see them frequently --- in my dreams; on waking, I would often see 4:19 on the alarm clock; while driving, cars in front of me would have the numbers 4 and 19; when driving through downtown Calgary, many times the large clock tower would read 4:19; and even until now, if I haven't checked my phone for a long period of time, I will pick it up and it reads 4:19 (either a.m. or p.m.!)! As a prophetic person, I knew that God was showing these numbers to me for a purpose, so I first searched every book of the Bible, from Genesis to Revelation, for what every Chapter 4 and Verse 19 read. (I even checked every Chapter 41:9 to make sure I hadn't misunderstood the numbers.)

For quite some time, I thought the only one that seemed to direct me as to what I should be doing is what one day jumped out at me while Bishop Oyedepo prayed. It was the reference to Matthew 4:19 (AMP) *And He said to them, Follow Me [as My disciples, accepting Me as your*

Master and Teacher and walking the same path of life that I walk], and I will make you fishers of men.

This was my understanding until December of 2020 when the Lord called me to plan a women's event, The Total Woman Conference which held in April of 2021, and the anchor Scripture reference He gave to me was Luke 4: 18 – 19! (AMPC)

The Spirit of the Lord [is] upon Me, because He has anointed Me [the Anointed One, the Messiah] <u>to preach</u> the good news (the Gospel) to the poor; He has sent Me to announce release to the captives and recovery of sight to the blind, to send forth as delivered those who are oppressed [who are downtrodden, bruised, crushed, and broken down by calamity],

<u>To proclaim</u> <u>the accepted</u> and <u>acceptable year of the Lord</u> [<u>the day</u> when salvation and the free favors of God profusely abound]. (underlining mine)

I saw it clearly, I understood my calling, another dimension of the miraculous; this is what God has raised me for! To declare, the accepted and acceptable **day**, not even the month; the **day** I declare this over somebody, it is done, when someone has an encounter with me.

On May 13th, 2022, in my deep sleep, I heard a loud voice, a clear voice, loudly, that stated, " You have been raised to speak to. and to open up the destinies of people." I woke up to look around for the person that spoke to me, but I didn't see anyone. I realized that it was a vision, so I wrote it down.

God was and has been allowing favor to speak in my life greatly, so that I can also dispense that favor to others.

I am praying over all these books, that each person who reads them will encounter the fall of the anointing for favor that has gone forth in prayer over each one.

Fola Sunny-Adeniyi

DEDICATION

I dedicate this book to God the Father, God the Son, and God the Holy Spirit. He alone is the giver and bestower of Favor. He not only favors me, He also raised me to declare His Favor upon His children.

ACKNOWLEDGMENTS

I wish to acknowledge, my beloved husband, (Pastor Sunny Adeniyi, Senior Pastor of Joy Overflow International Church in Calgary) for his mentorship and guidance while writing this book. Thank you so much; you're the best husband any woman could ask for! I love you!

A big thank you to my mother, Mrs. Banke Shonubi, for instilling in me the discipline and fear of God since my childhood. I love you dearly, Mum.

I also would like to say a very big thank you to Mama Ruth Yesmaniski for her time, effort, and skill in putting this book together. Her patience is that of an angel, her expertise is unparalleled. Thank you so much, ma. Love you.

There are so many friends, mentors and members of my family, both biological and 'adopted' that I would like to mention and appreciate, for their expressions of love and support to me over the years: my beloved father-in-love, Rev. Phillip Adeniyi -- love you Daddy!; my grandma of faith, Arch Bishop Margaret Benson-Idahosa – thank you ma for bringing me into your family, ma, I love you dearly!; my mentors in the prophetic -- Pst. P.K. Olawale and Pst. Mrs. Bolanle Olawale—thank you sir and ma; my fathers in the Lord – Pst. Dele Bamgboye and Apostle Kingsley Ike – God bless you sirs; my mamas in the Lord – Rev. Funke Felix Adejumo, Pst. Mrs. Dele Bamgboye, Pst. Kofo Babatunde, Pst. Imade Alabi –God bless you all, love you all Mas.

Much appreciation to my beloved uncles, Mr. Segun Odumosu and Mr. lawale Odumosu, especially for your unrelenting support and love for me -- God bless you richly in Jesus' Name, sirs!

My sisters and brothers, Sola, Funmi, Oke, Hon. Bolaji, Dr. Kemi, Ife, Inem, Ruth, Mr. A, Pst. Titi, Dr. Tope, Seyi, Sola son, Bunmi, Yemi-- God bless you all -- love you all! I also want to thank and appreciate ALL my Joy Overflow International Calgary church family represented by Dcn. Joseph Ogidan and Sis Opeyemi Fasoyiro; Thank you ALL so much! Love you all!

I also appreciate all my T.T.W.C. (The Total Woman) Conference members worldwide. Much love to all.

In addition, I would like to appreciate my beloved friends-turned-sisters Dupe, Tola, Dcns Lola, Oge, Sade, Njide, Sis Bola, Minister Wunmi, Sis Jane, Kike, Sis Deedee, Pst. Dee, Sis Ify, Juli, Evelyn, Dr. Wunmi, Sis Joy, Dcns Remi, Bola, Regina and all my sisters worldwide. Love you all so dearly.

My Aunties; Aunty Akinsanya, Aunty Moji Taiwo, Aunty Allen, Aunty Tosin, and all my Aunties all over, love you all Mas.

Finally, I wish to acknowledge the business owners used by God; thank you for allowing God to use you to be a part of 'My Favor Testimonies'. God bless you and your businesses.

Jeff Farr

Farr Furnace and Air Conditioning Ltd
612 38 Street S.W. Calgary, Alberta T3C 1T2

Kiuris Silva
K & J General Construction Inc.
67 - 32 Whitnel Court NE   Calgary, Alberta T1Y 5E3

Rajdeep Grewal
Sapphire Lighting
2003-39 Avenue N.E. Calgary, Alberta   T2E 6R7

Ben Ben
Metro Cabinets
5074 80 Avenue SE, Unit B   Calgary, Alberta T2C 2X3

TABLE OF CONTENTS

Psalm 84:11

For the Lord God is a Sun and Shield; the Lord bestows [present] grace *and* favor and [future] glory (honor, splendor, and heavenly bliss)! No good thing will He withhold from those who walk uprightly.

Psalm 90:17

And let the beauty and delightfulness *and* favor of the Lord our God be upon us; confirm *and* establish the work of our hands – yes, the work of our hands, confirm *and* establish it.

MIRACLE DEBT CANCELLATION

When my husband and I were planning to move from our home country of Nigeria to Canada, we had to find a solution for payment of a mortgage that we still carried on our investment building. The bank had given us a loan to the tune of 8.9 million Naira back in 2002. We also added our own money to the mortgage amount to buy our very first investment property. In 2007, by the Lord's leading, we were instructed to move to Canada for an assignment the Lord had for us. Back in 2002, when we obtained the mortgage for the investment property, part of the collateral the bank required was our school certificates, to which effect, my husband submitted his own.

However, now in 2007 when we wanted to come to Canada, we realized we would need to get my husband's certificates from the bank in order to be integrated into the Canadian immigration system.

We approached the bank representative, and she advised the only condition to get them back was for my husband to pay back the remaining amount on the mortgage loan; then they would release the documents of the house and my husband's certificates to us. All this time, they had retained the original documents of the house awaiting our full loan repayment before handing the documents over to us.

When we calculated how much we needed to pay to the bank to satisfy the debt, it totaled about 7.8 million Naira. To us, at that time, this was HUGE! We didn't have sufficient funds in our account, so we put up another investment property for sale. Within 11 days or thereabouts, the property was sold for even a higher amount than what it had been listed for. First *miracle.*

We sowed a seed of 10% of the proceeds to God in thanks for the house sale, for the favor and speed of it.

The following week my husband approached the Human Resources department at the bank to pay back the remaining amount on the mortgage loan to them, so he could collect the original documents and his certificates. On opening the system to confirm our balance, it was showing that our account balance left to be paid was ZERO!! My husband protested that he was sure we still had a balance to pay but the HR manager insisted it was fully paid. My husband was referred to the executive director in charge of Human Resources and once there, told her the same story; that our balance should be around 7.8 million Naira. The director stated "Unfortunately, our system says otherwise, so we have to follow the system, so you don't sue us in the future." Because of the seemingly bizarre circumstances, my husband too insisted that the department should write a formal letter to that effect, stating that we were no longer owing them. The letter was written with the bank's stamp on it! They also immediately gave my husband his certificates and the original documents too! In summary, considering that out of 8.9 million borrowed with a remaining balance of 7.8 million owing for a 4plex building (a building with four flats), we can almost conclude that God gave us a free house! Hallelujah!

Isn't our GOD FAITHFUL and AMAZING??

The favor of God is real indeed!!!

1 Samuel 16:22

Saul sent to Jesse, Saying, Let David remain in my service, for he pleases me.

Psalm 5:12

For You, Lord, will bless the [uncompromisingly] righteous [him who is upright and in right standing with You]; as with a shield You will surround him with goodwill (pleasure and favor).

MIRACLE JOB

Our move from Africa to Canada successfully took place in 2007. We settled in Calgary, Alberta (the place of the mountains that God had clearly called us to). Within around a month of our landing, I got a job as a cashier. The pay was not so much but nevertheless, I was grateful to God and was always happy on the job. However, after about three months of working there, I desired to get into a career, not just a job.

Prior to coming to Canada, I had a conversation with God and asked, "Please Lord, let your promise to me in the book of Isaiah 48:17 be fulfilled."

Thus saith the LORD, thy Redeemer, the Holy One of Israel; I am the LORD thy God which teacheth thee to profit, which leadeth thee by the way that thou shouldest go.

Isaiah 48:17 (KJV)

"No matter what certificate I have, lead me in your own will for my life in this new country."

The Lord heard me and began to lead me Himself.

Still on the current job, I wanted more… specifically, the ability to buy a house. Everybody kept telling me, that it was not possible. So I confided in my HR manager who happened to be very fond of me. She told me that she could only move me to another department but the pay still wouldn't be fantastic in order for my husband and I to get a mortgage that quickly. But she moved me anyways.

One day while I was at work, my Admin Manager pulled me aside and said that a friend of hers had just told her that morning that they are hiring a staff that would be in charge of a vault at another company. She cautioned that I shouldn't let anyone know she told me, but she would hate to see me go.

I thanked her and went to the said company the following day. When I got to the customer service, one of the ladies there offered me a form to fill for my job application request. As I was about to fill out the form, another lady tapped me from behind and asked if I was there for the vault position.

I said "Yes."

She directed my eyes to another woman and said "That's the Assistant General Manager, why don't you go talk to her yourself about this job?"

So I walked up to the wonderful lady who was not only beautiful but equally kind. She received me with a smile and asked what she could do for me. So I responded that I had come to apply for the vault position.

She said "Oh that" with a smile.

So she changed the whole discussion and asked if I was a graduate, and I said "Yes."

She further questioned, "Great, what did you study?"

I told her computer science but that I was enrolled at Athabasca University currently, studying physiology. What I didn't know at that point was that she heard 'psychology'. Unknown to me, there was a new position opening up at the company, requiring the candidate to be a college graduate with a psychology background. She sent me home to bring my resume and submit it to apply for the Project Coordinator position. She explained that I didn't need any experience or expertise because I would be trained on the job.

I went home, brought back my resume, and was called in for an interview about 3 days later.

Guess what?

During the interview, a question came up in regard to their expectation that the potential employee must have a psychology background. The Assistant

General Manager was one of the interviewers and she interjected on my behalf, before I had a chance to respond, stating "Oh she's studying psychology at the moment so she's qualified."

I didn't say a word, even though I knew she heard me wrongly because I had told her I was studying physiology and she heard psychology.

A day later I got the job. God elevated me and made me the best of the best.

Isn't our God AMAZING!!!

The Favor of God is real indeed!!!

Esther 2: 8-9

So when the king's command and his decree were proclaimed and when many maidens were gathered in Shushan the capital under the custody of Hegai, Esther also was taken to the king's house into the custody of Hegai, keeper of the women.

And the maiden pleased [Hegai] and obtained his favor. And he speedily gave her the things for her purification and her portion of food and the seven chosen maids to be given her from the king's palace; and he removed her and her maids to the best [apartment] in the harem.

Daniel 1:9

Now God made Daniel to find favor, compassion, *and* loving-kindness with the chief of the eunuchs,

MIRACLE HOME

This particular testimony began when I was desperate to buy a house. My husband and I had decided to drive to the community where we desired to live and parked on the street of a beautiful neighborhood. We then removed our shoes, got out of the car and started walking up and down the street declaring,*"Every place whereon the soles of your feet shall tread shall be yours: from the wilderness and Lebanon, from the river, the river Euphrates, even unto the uttermost sea shall your coast be."*(Deuteronomy 11:24 KJV)

and

"Moses my servant is dead; now therefore arise, go over this Jordan, thou, and all this people, unto the land which I do give to them, even to the children of Israel. Every place that the sole of your foot shall tread upon, that have I given unto you, as I said unto Moses. From the wilderness and this

Lebanon even unto the great river, the river Euphrates, all the land of the Hittites, and unto the great sea toward the going down of the sun, shall be your coast. There shall not any man be able to stand before thee all the days of thy life: as I was with Moses, so I will be with thee: I will not fail thee, nor forsake thee. "(Joshua 1:2-5 KJV)

The people that may have noticed us that day might very well have questioned what we were doing as this was in the winter, snow was on the ground, *and* we were new in Canada. We had only been in Calgary for maybe a month!

All we knew was that we loved the look of the houses in that particular estate area. When we told friends about the type of house we wanted, we were told by them that before we could afford houses like that we must have stayed in Canada for most likely at least 15 years with a very good six-figure salary job. They were rightfully wrong.

Don't get me wrong, they are our good friends, and were just watching out for us and saying the obvious in the natural. They actually stated the facts, but not the Truth.

Anyways we began to contact realtors and mortgage specialists and they were approving us for about one fifth of what our choice houses cost. I kept changing realtors but I never gave up on God's Word and promises. I kept telling the realtors to take me to houses in the areas where I wanted. By this time I had located other estates that I found might even be better than where we initially stepped our feet on.

In our seventh month in Calgary, a shift came. I got a new job, and surprisingly my husband too got a new job.

Meanwhile, a week before he got that job, I had gone with another realtor, and I saw this one beautiful home listed for sale. I told the realtor "This is my home."

He looked at me like I was crazy because he had already calculated how much the bank would approve us for and we would be $450,000 short of what the house was listed for. So we left.

By the following week, my husband got a new job paying him a six-figure salary, coupled with my new job.

When we attended church that Sunday where my husband gave his testimony of the new job, a lady stopped to talk to me after the service. She said "Fola now that Sunny has a new job, can we take a look at your mortgage again?" I said "Yes, although we know the banks would need about 3 to 6 months' probation time before approval." She then said "Don't worry about it, I am the bank manager, and we trust you and Sunny. Please come have coffee with me tomorrow."

Lo and behold, her husband too had just gotten a job as a mortgage specialist and head for that bank in our city! He joined us for the hang out and before we left them, our mortgage was approved! I called the realtor to let him know we were approved for $50,000 dollars less than what the seller wanted for the house. He was shocked to hear that we were approved for so close to the selling price but even so, he said he had been a realtor for years and in that time there's no one who had reduced $50,000 from their asking price before. I told him, "Go, make the offer, we will be the first. Just go." The guy came back overwhelmed that the owner had accepted the offer. Praise the Lord!!!

We moved into that house exactly 9 months after we came to Canada. God's Favor is so real!!!The location alone was more beautiful than the place where we first trod our feet on. The house is more beautiful than what I wanted too. What's more is that the previous owners were the first occupants and had only lived there for a year before we bought it so the house was practically new. What more? The previous owners must have spent a fortune on the gardens, both at the back and at the front. The house came with big trees, big rocks and beautiful landscaping.

Isn't our God an AWESOME God?

The Favor of God is real indeed!!!

Genesis 19:19

Behold now, your servant has found favor in your sight, and you have magnified your kindness and mercy to me in saving my life; but I cannot escape to the mountains, lest the evil overtake me, and I die.

Genesis 18:3

And said, My lord, if now I have found favor in your sight, do not pass by your servant, I beg of you.

MIRACLE OF BEAUTIFUL THINGS

God's miracles come in all shapes and sizes!

This testimony is about the time when I wanted to change the chandeliers in our home.

I went to a lighting store here in Calgary to modernize the lighting in our house. I picked out two chandeliers; they were stunning, big and costly! The owner said he would see what he could do to reduce the prices for me and left it at that. They imported the beautiful lighting pieces from the USA to Canada.

When they got to my house, three workers came, they unpacked the chandeliers installed them and also helped to fix the kitchen island pendant lightings and then left. I was expecting my bill which was in multiples of four figures, but I waited and waited, and they didn't send it. I finally called them about it to ask why I hadn't received the billing yet.

The guy only replied, "Don't bother yourself."

It has been 2 years now!

To God alone be the glory!!!!

The Favor of God is real indeed!!!

Genesis 39:21

But the Lord was with Joseph, and showed him mercy and loving-kindness and gave him favor in the sight of the warden of the prison.

Genesis 39:4

So Joseph pleased [Potiphar] *and* found favor in his sight, and he served him. And [his master] made him supervisor over his house and he put all that he had in his charge.

MIRACLE RENOVATIONS

In 2020, when I was about to celebrate my 50th birthday, I was actually trying to renovate some parts of my house before the celebration as I knew I would be entertaining guests.

One of the major changes I wanted to work on was the cabinets and countertops throughout the house. I was hoping to change them from laminate counter tops to quartz or granite.

I contacted a contractor who I had never met before. After speaking with him, he came to measure my whole house for the replacements I had requested, but when he gave me the quote for my kitchen, I knew I wouldn't be able to do the rest of my house, which included the guest washroom upstairs, and the washroom in the master bedroom, which has a 'his and hers' vanity. We also needed to replace the three sinks in these washrooms. The kitchen cost alone, which was a couple of thousand dollars, was quite a reasonable cost. As a former building contractor, I knew pricing very well. Given the cost versus what we had budgeted, we settled for my kitchen cabinets, granite countertop and the kitchen island countertop.

When this contractor came back to the house, he asked if I wanted to do the granite counter tops for the washrooms upstairs. I said "Yes, but I don't think I want to do it now because of the cost." I stated that doing them would definitely cost close to what the kitchen estimate was or maybe even more. He looked at me and said something surprising and shocking; he told me to go and pick the granite slab and design I want from a particular company, and he gave me the address. He said he then would see if he had the exact same design in his warehouse that he also sells to his customers.

So off I went to get the design I wanted, sent it to his phone and we were able to find something close to the design at his warehouse that I picked for the kitchen countertop and also for the upstairs washrooms. But the amazing thing was that the design I found at his warehouse was quartz!!! It was more beautiful and of higher quality than the granite. Then he said something astonishing; he said, "The material, workmanship, transportation, installation etc. is on me. Don't worry about it." He asked if I would like to change the sinks too or use the old sinks, I told him I would like new sinks. He said "I don't sell those, but I'll go to my suppliers to grab them for you. Just add $200 to my earlier quote, one sink should cost that, $200." I was shocked and couldn't believe my ears and eyes. This could only be God!

I also upgraded my kitchen sink to the big industrial-like sink at no extra cost. All my kitchen got completed, beautifully well done, excellent top-notch finishing. And my upstairs washrooms countertops too, done perfectly.

God's favor is real!!!!

Now there's a catch to this testimony. The lady that introduced me to this guy, when I gave her the testimony, she said *now* she believed that this was favor indeed. Apparently the fellow was really angry with her over $150 he demanded from her for just helping her to fix or cut something out of her cabinet. That same guy, threw in all these bonuses, worth thousands of dollars, for me???

Isn't God amazing? His love endures forever!!!

The Favor of God is real indeed!!!

Luke 1:20

Now behold, you will be *and* will continue to be silent and not able to speak till the day when these things take place, because you have not believed what I told you; but my words are of a kind which will be fulfilled in the appointed *and* proper time.

Isaiah 49:8

Thus says the Lord, In the acceptable *and* favorable time I have heard *and* answered you, and in a day of salvation I have helped you; and I will preserve you and give you for a covenant to the people, to raise up *and* establish the land [from its present state of ruin] and to apportion *and* cause them to inherit the desolate [moral wasted of heathenism, their] heritages.

ANOTHER MIRACLE RENOVATION

The previous testimony brings me to this next one.

I wanted to change the design of my kitchen island, because the former one was double layered. But for a new look, I wanted a single, flat surface look.

I called a kitchen cabinet contractor to give me a quote for the upgrade I had in mind, and I exchanged pictures with him and dimensions. We only spoke over the phone, but he sent his worker to do the work. He had to dismantle the faucet, the sink, and the countertop of the cabinet before he could cut the extra layer off. He spent several hours in my house, to cut that layer off and to fix back all the things he had removed.

When he was done, I called the main contractor to ask what the price would be.

He answered me, "Your fee is zero."

I was like "No! You're kidding me!" to which he calmly responded, "No, I'm not."

Isn't this God worth serving?

The Favor of God is real indeed!!!

Isaiah 58:11

And the Lord shall guide you continually and satisfy you in drought *and* in dry places and make strong your bones. And you shall be like a watered garden and like a spring of water whose waters fail not.

John 1:16

For out of His fullness (abundance) we have all received [all had a share and we were all supplied with] one grace after another *and* spiritual blessing upon spiritual blessing *and* even favor upon favor *and* gift [heaped] upon gift.

ONE MORE MIRACLE RENOVATION

This testimony is short but sweet......

2020 was a year we won't soon forget considering how the whole world was turned upside down because of something that was unprecedented. By the first week of March, Covid 19 impacted Canada and although we first thought it would be something that passed as quickly as it had begun, it became evident that my plans for my 50th birthday to do some home renovations in order to accommodate guests would no longer be necessary due to 'gathering restrictions', even though we had done much already.

But.... that didn't mean we weren't going to have some sort of celebration! In order to follow some of the gathering mandates issued by the government, we decided to do a drive through party.

My driveway would be beautifully decorated, and I would sit there, while people would drive by and I would wave to them.

However, there was a need to paint my garage door!

When I called the painter and explained the plan, he said, "I'll do this for free for you, just grab the paint color you want and I'll paint your garage for free!!!!"

I couldn't believe my ears! But true to his word, the painter gifted me with the painting of my garage door!

This God of heaven just decided to dazzle and pamper me!!!

The Favor of God is real indeed!!!

.

Joshua 1:8

This Book of the Law shall not depart out of your mouth, but you shall meditate on it day and night, that you may observe *and* do according to all that is written in it. For then you shall make your way prosperous, and then you shall deal wisely *and* have good success.

Luke 2:52

And Jesus increased in wisdom (in broad and full understanding) and in stature *and* years, and in favor with God and man.

MIRACLE OF FREE SUNGLASSES

The Lord has favored me numerous times when shopping for items which I went to buy at stores, for many years, by getting them for free.

I went to a 'highbrow' shop just to do some window shopping, but this particular day, the owner was around. To my surprise I found a pair of designer sunglasses, which I had been looking for, for quite some time but had always avoided buying them at the big malls because of the price.

When I found them that day, because the owner was there, I began to negotiate the price with her. She finally looked at me and stated, "You like them."

I said "Yes, I do."

She surprised me by saying "You can have them, for free."

I was beyond excited and astonished at the same time.

The Favor of God is real indeed!!!

Judges 6:17

Gideon said to Him, If now I have found favor in Your sight, then show me a sign that it is You Who talks with me.

Malachi 1:11

For from the rising of the sun to its setting My name shall be great among the nations, and in every place incense shall be offered to My name, and indeed a pure offering; for My name shall be great among the nations, says the Lord of hosts.

MIRACLE CLUTCH

Another time I came upon a high-end shoe store in one of the biggest shopping centres in Calgary - Chinook Mall.

When I got inside the store, I noticed that they didn't have anything that I was looking for, only expensive shoes and clutch bags. However, a particular bag caught my eye before I turned to leave, so I sat down to really admire the clutch; but definitely not to buy it. As God would have it, I think the owner of this particular store chain was visiting this one of their many stores, so he came up to me and asked, "You like that?"

I said, "Yes but it's too expensive."

He continued by asking me how much I had in my hand. I told him that I had only stopped by to look for slip-ons because my foot was hurting, and I couldn't go much further in the shoes I was wearing. I had decided to stop at the nearest shoe shop, which just happened to be this one since I was looking for a pair of comfortable slip-ons. I only had a budget for that.

He asked again how much I had and so I told him. The next thing I knew he told one of the workers waiting on me to wrap the beautiful purse and give it to me.

I opened my mouth but couldn't say a word! The clerk that had been waiting on me and my husband said, "I have worked here for 5 years, and I have never seen this before!"

I must say, for all of these "blessing" encounters, my husband was always a witness.

The Favor of God is real indeed!!!

Acts 7:10

And delivered him from all distressing afflictions and won him goodwill *and* favor and wisdom *and* understanding in the sight of Pharaoh, king of Egypt and all his house.

Psalm 30:5

For His anger is but for a moment, but His favor is for a lifetime or in His favor is life. Weeping may endure for a night, but joy comes in the morning.

MIRACLE HANDBAG

Recently, one of my daughters in the Lord travelled to Italy and bought a beautiful designer handbag for herself.

On getting back home to Canada, the Holy Spirit spoke to her saying, "That's Pastor Fola's bag, give it to her."

She argued saying "But God, I already bought her the perfume from this trip."; and left it at that.

She then went ahead to carry the bag to church on Sunday and the Holy Spirit said again, "Give it to Pastor Fola." She said "No, I won't."

When she got home the Holy Spirit once more said, "You are carrying Pastor Fola's bag."

On Monday morning, when she went to the washroom, the Holy Spirit insisted, "Take that bag to Pastor Fola."

Needless to say, I was surprised to get downstairs from our bedroom on Monday, very early in the morning, to meet this beautiful handbag waiting for me.

If that is not God's favor I don't know what else it is!

The Favor of God is real indeed!!!

Proverbs 12:2

A good man obtains favor from the Lord, but a man of wicked devices He condemns.

Psalm 102:13

You will arise *and* have mercy *and* loving-kindness for Zion, for it is time to have pity *and* compassion for her; yes, the set time has come [the moment designated]

MIRACLE FASHION EARRINGS

Another shopping adventure took us to another mall in our city where I entered a gift store that sells pearl jewelry and various other gifts.

I had gone there to buy a gift for a friend. After picking her gift, as I was on my way to pay, I spotted a pair of gorgeous pearl and crystal earrings.

I turned to my husband and said "Wowww! These would be perfect for my dress and would match my pearl necklace….. but it's too pricy."

The sales lady actually heard me say it and came to me and asked if I liked the earrings.

I replied "Yes, I do."

The next thing she did, without saying a word, was she took them off the shelf, put them in a beautiful box and said "They're yours….. for free!"

Wowwww.!!!!   God is ever faithful!!!

The Favor of God is real indeed!!!

Psalm 106:4

[Earnestly] remember me, O Lord, when You favor Your people! O visit me also when You deliver them, *and* grant me Your salvation! --

Romans 6:14

For sin shall not [any longer] exert dominion over you, since now you are not under Law [as slaves], but under grace [as subjects of God's favor and mercy].

MIRACLE CAR LOAN PAYOFF

A few years back, I had a Honda Odyssey van that we bought brand new in 2007. It was a good vehicle and never broke down once, but the mileage on it was getting higher very quickly. In 2017 there was a heavy hailstorm which caused damage to the car because of the size of the hailstones. Honestly, I was not too happy about it because nothing of mine gets tampered with by the devil. So, I was asked to turn the van in for inspection for an insurance claim because of the hail damage,

I was actually surprised when the report came back that my van was a write off and I was to be given a certain amount as compensation to get a new car. It was a shock because the damage was only on the roof but there was none on the body of the van.

A few days later the cheque was given to me, which was for a reasonable amount, but my van was taken, so I asked the insurance company if I could buy my van back from them. The adjuster said no as it's against their policy. The lady I was talking to then secretly gave me a number and told me to call the company, to see if they could help me. The company was the company that buys damaged cars from the insurance company. When I called them, initially they were hesitant. I called the insurance lady back and told her their response. She then said, "you know what, I'm going to give your case an exemption." She ended up giving me the cheque for the van and allowed me to buy my van back at a minimal cost.

I couldn't believe my eyes or ears! I got the cheque, repaired my van for about $300 and was able to sell it undamaged at the market rate.

Combined, the cheque money and the van sale money were enough to allow me to buy a new GMC Acadia SUV

God works in mysterious ways!!

The Favor of God is real indeed!!!

Ruth 2:10

Then she fell on her face, bowing to the ground, and said to him, Why have I found favor in your eyes that you should notice me, when I am a foreigner?

Romans 6:14

For sin shall not [any longer] exert dominion over you, since now you are not under Law [as slaves], but under grace [as subjects of God's favor and mercy].

MIRACLES OF STRANGE FAVORS

There are so many times I have walked into strange favors that I can give full account of in my life such as the following ….

This particular testimony is about the favor I enjoyed as a building and renovation contractor and also as an event planner and decorator.

God favored me with the best contractors and workers, since starting my own businesses. I never recorded a deficit or loss on any project, and I never experienced any law suits against my company or myself to the glory of God! We never recorded a single accident or injury on any of my job sites or event venues.

Most of my former contractors are now like family to me to the extent that if I call them for a service in my home, they don't charge me any money!

At one point during this time in my life, I increased my tithing to 20% and God made sure I always had projects on the go. Once I had about seven or eight projects running concurrently, and God finished them well for me. When my husband went into full time Ministry in 2015, without any pay from the church we were pastoring then, God expanded my businesses so much that all my tithes were in five figures in Canadian dollars. Even though my husband was not on salary, we had an abundance of cash flow and were able to effortlessly support and help the ministries God had used us to pioneer, to the glory of God!

My boast in the Lord as a contractor and an event decorator is that God made me the best in my field!

The Favor of God is real indeed!!!

Exodus 3:21

And I will give this people favor *and* respect in the sight of the Egyptians; and it shall be that when you go, you shall not go empty-handed.

Exodus 33:17

And I have declared that I will bring you up out of the affliction of Egypt to the land of the Canaanite, the Hittite, the Amorite, the Perizzite, the Hivite, and the Jebusite, to a land flowing with milk and honey.

DEBT CANCELLATION # 2

Who says God can't do things more than once, even for the same person???And even better than before???

In 2010, I began my first entrepreneurial enterprise; an event decorating business, while I was still employed as a Project Coordinator. I had found a niche that needed advancement when I planned and decorated for my 40th birthday party. Coming from Africa, Nigerians celebrate special occasions in grand style, with elaborate decorations, plenty of food and a large number of guests. I found that I was able to envision and co-ordinate my event with more ease, precision and flair than using any of the available service providers at that time. By the time my party was over, I had numerous guests wanting me to plan their event decorations too, and that's how that venture began!

Now that we are here, do you recall my prayer to God before coming to Canada, where I asked for His leading and He provided me with the miracle job of a Project Coordinator? Well, in 2013, that job became the seed for my second entrepreneurial undertaking which led me to become the owner of a very successful construction company. God had made these businesses lucrative, thriving and stress free. He made sure that I had the best tradesmen and women working for me in that construction company and conscientious helpers in the event decorating business. (To this day I continue to recommend those workers to people who still ask for quality workers.)

Strangely enough, and quite suddenly and unexpectedly, in 2019 the Lord called me into full time ministry to work with my husband who equally became a full-time pastor. It was a very tough step for me because my businesses were doing very well but obediently I dropped everything and started working for the ministry without a salary up until today.

Although I was offered compensation, I was just not comfortable with collecting salary from the church.

I need to let you know, the income from my businesses was our main income. We did have a healthy sum of money of our own saved up, but in 2018 a need arose for my Mum back in Nigeria. We desired to buy her a new property in a gated community. This new home for her cost us six figures in Canadian dollars as well as the cost of purchasing and transporting all the furniture for my mother's new accommodation from Canada, which was paid out of our savings. We also bought a pre-owned Honda Sienna for my father-in-law.

At that time, we were sure of making the money back through my businesses but that was not to be when God called me to step away from the businesses. When I   closed down the businesses, we gradually began to spend from our savings. From the beginning of that year to the end, we had spent all of our savings.

When my construction company was hired for some government projects, it had required me to start up with my own money which was then reimbursed by the company after passing inspections at different phases of completion. In order to do this, the bank had provided me with a six-figure business operating line of credit. I had never paid interest on that loan because I had only used it for business purposes.

I also had another five-figure loan from another bank for my businesses as well as five figure credit cards from the two banks. The truth is that I never defaulted on the loans or credit card payments all through the period of actively running the businesses.

But…. We had to dip our hands into that loan just to make ends meet. Between the spring of 2019 and the summer of 2020, I had dipped my hand into the loans I was given by the bank to support the home front and the other responsibilities we needed money for. I maxed out on the loans and credit cards. I was also used to supporting and helping a lot of poor families in Africa. I did not stop; the monetary gifts I get from ministering and seeds sown into my life, I was using to help the families and orphanage homes, widows help groups, and cerebral palsy care groups. During Covid, in 2020, I took all of my monetary gifts and raised funds to buy food and groceries for the less privileged to support them in Africa. We actually had about 4 major outreaches then, in 2 major cities in Africa.

But the bank loan was what I was using to support and spend on the home front, until I maxed out my credit cards and loans. Not long after, I began to default on the interest payments too. So, one day, being tired of only paying monthly interest, I called the bank where I had the bigger loan. I was told by the person I spoke to that I would have to file for bankruptcy if my loan was not forgiven. I let them know that I could sell my event business inventory which was worth about $30,000. So that I could pay back part of the loan from the proceeds, to which they agreed. They then referred me to a loan consolidation company.

When I called the company and explained my situation to the woman, she said with excitement "My son is also a pastor and I know the plight of some pastors."

Long story short, God consolidated my loan through her. I did not have to file for bankruptcy, they reduced the loan; up to about $40,000 was cancelled by the second bank, the debt to the first bank with the six-figure loan and credit card was also cancelled and I was asked to pay back $30,000 within 5 years.

In summary, I believe the person assigned to my case must have been arranged by God supernaturally because:

1.God used her to cancel my big loan which was a six-figure loan

2.God used her to cancel my second loan which was approximately $40,000

3. Almost all of my loan was written off except for $30,000 which I was to pay back within 5 years *and* the Lord intervened again about the remaining payback.

4. Around the same period, the Lord paid off the remaining amount owing of approximately $23,000 on my SUV (the initial amount I paid to buy the SUV Acadia was just part of the full cost of the vehicle.)

And what's more, God did another amazing thing in all of this!

Remember the $30,000 I was to pay back to the bank from the sale of my business inventory? They no longer demanded for this again in the final documents! So I sold the inventory and the proceeds were mine.

Instead of going to sell the items individually on Kijiji or marketplace God made arrangement for them to be bought all at once. By the end of December 2020, somebody called to buy all my event business items, and I sold them all; at a ridiculously cheap price, and still cut off almost half the cost after the discounted price. Just remembering how God paid off my huge loan made me to bless somebody else, to start off their own business. The inventory cost for my business items after discount was about $30,000 so I asked the person to pay $15,000. I paid my blessing forward.

Today to the glory of God, I have just one bank card in my purse which is a Visa debit card.

Isn't our God AMAZING!!!

The Favor of God is real indeed!!!

Psalm 68:19

Blessed be the Lord, Who bears our burdens *and* carries us day by day, even the God Who is our salvation! *Selah* [pause, and calmly think of that]!

Luke 4:19

To proclaim the accepted and acceptable year of the Lord [the day when salvation and the free favors of God profusely abound].

MIRACLE TRAVEL FAVOR

Some time ago, my husband and I had a stop-over in Houston, Texas.

We had started the boarding process to our final destination and several people had already boarded ahead of us. When it got to our turn, the boarding agent asked if we would love to be in business class. You can imagine the excitement that glowed on our faces!

She disposed of the boarding passes we had in our hands and changed them to business class, asking us to only pay $30 extra! We were so dumbfounded. When we entered the plane, we saw that it was a full flight. We knew that the favor of God was working when we realized we were the only people offered that opportunity.

The Favor of God is real indeed!!!

Another miracle flight favor happened in October of 2022.

My husband and I were on our way back to Canada from the USA after a brief visit. The several flights in a short period of time before this last transfer flight had caused both of my feet to swell, because of flying for long hours. When we got to our boarding gate, one of the boarding attendants approached me and asked if I would want to go ahead of everyone. She could see I was 'dragging' my feet and I said "Yes, I wouldn't mind".

I stretched forth my feet to show her why I was having the difficulty in walking.

She said nothing but came back a few minutes later, gave us new boarding passes and tore the old ones.

Lo and behold, when we got into the plane. we realized we had been moved from the normal economy to extra leg room which is called "Premium

Seating" on Air Canada. From flight reviews, Air Canada's Premium Seating is the best upscale amongst the airlines. Normally, a person would need to pay from $130 or more per person for the upgrade. As if that was not enough, the lady made sure that there was nobody sitting between my husband and I, so I could really have space to stretch. My husband and I looked around and saw that this plane was also packed full, there were no empty seats except the one between us. She came back to check on me and made sure I was comfortable before stepping out of the plane.

I thanked her and offered her a clutch purse that I had with me as an appreciation for what she had done, but she declined it. With a broad smile she said something before stepping out, "Thank you so much for making my years."

I didn't understand it, but I thanked her too and she alighted from the plane before we took off.

The Favor of God is real indeed!!!

Proverbs 12:2 (TPT)

If your heart is right, favor flows from the Lord, but a devious heart invites his condemnation.

Psalm 89:17 (TPT)

The glory of your splendor is our strength, and your marvelous favor makes us even stronger, lifting us even higher!

MIRACLE PROVISION FAVORS

This is a testimony of multiple favor over many years!

When we moved to Calgary with my husband, at one point, we needed a certain amount of money to show in our bank account so we could be approved for our first mortgage. Though we had over a hundred thousand dollars in our account, the realtor I was dealing with told me if the bank saw this certain amount in our account, they would consider us to approve the mortgage. Since we didn't have the remaining balance available, I approached a family member, who has been so very, very dear to me, about it. With no further ado, he sent me the remaining $15,000 I needed. Eventually the deal did not go through, so I wanted to send the money back to him. He said, I should hold on to the money, I might need it in the future, as we had just recently moved to Calgary.

A few years later, I needed to develop our basement which I just mentioned to him. He asked how much more money did I need to do it. I told him $12,000 which he sent without hesitating, though we agreed it was as a loan. There were two times that I needed Naira back in Nigeria, I had dollars, but needed 1 million Naira one time, at another time, 1.2 million Naira. He sent them to my account and told me not to bother sending the dollars equivalent back to him.

There have been several other blessings like that, I have enjoyed from him; he has the largest heart amongst all my family members. He's good to every one of us. I was thinking because he blesses other family members that it was just a normal thing with him.

But this year I was sharing the testimonies of his large heart with my chief bridesmaid, and she said something remarkable. She asked " Fola, don't you think, it's this favor that's upon your life, that's making him to bless you in that manner? Has he given these large amounts to any of your siblings?"

It was as if a light bulb went on in my head, and I acknowledged God, that truly it's the favor of God upon my life that's making him to go extra miles for me.

The Favor of God is real indeed!!!

I decree, in the Name of Jesus, from this moment forward, I see myself the way God sees me.

I am highly favored of the Lord; I am crowned with glory and honor.

I am the righteousness of God in Christ Jesus

I am reigning as a king/queen in life through the one man, Jesus Christ, the Messiah.

Now, in Jesus' Name, I declare by faith that I walk in divine favor.

I have preferential treatment, supernatural increase.

I have restoration.

I have prominence.

I have petitions granted, laws changed, policies and rules changed, and battles won which I do not have to fight. Why? All because of favor.

The blessing and favor of God is on my life.

In Jesus Name, every morning, when I arise, I will speak and expect divine favor to go before me and surround me as with a shield, with goodwill and pleasures forevermore.

Doors are now open for me that men said are impossible to open.

No obstacles can stop me, no hindrances can delay me.

In Jesus Name, I am honored by my Father, as I receive genuine favor that comes directly from God.

I am special to Him, I am the object of His affection, I am the apple of His eyes, I am blessed and highly favored of the Lord.

Everyone and everything shall work to favor me.

God's Goodness and Mercy shall accompany me in all my ways.

So shall it be for me and my household today in Jesus' Name. AMEN and AMEN!

TRIGGERS OF GOD'S FAVOR

The favor of God is for every child of God. According to the book of Ephesians 1:11 *"In him we have obtained an inheritance, having been predestined according to the purpose of him who works all things according to the counsel of his will."*

Part of our inheritances in Christ is Favor according to the afore-mentioned Scripture but we need to be in Christ before we can access these inheritances. Favor is therefore a free gift of God but there are certain steps to take to trigger God's favor.

The following are some of those triggers of favor.

1. Get Saved

Give your life to Jesus Christ. Surrender your life to Christ, allow Jesus Christ to be the Aleph and the Tav of your life.(Alpha and Omega)

II Corinthians 5:17 *Therefore if any person is [ingrafted] in Christ (the Messiah) he is a new creation (a new creature altogether); the old [previously moral and spiritual condition] has passed away. Behold, the fresh* and *new has come!*

2.   Get baptized with the Holy Spirit

Acts 1:8 *But you shall receive power (ability, efficiency, and might)when the Holy Spirit has come upon you, and you shall be My witnesses in Jerusalem and all Judea and Samaria and to the ends (the very bounds) of the earth.*

3.   Develop a deeper and closer walk with God and walk righteously

God only bestows favor on those who love and walk with Him. Despite people's opinion, make sure you are walking righteously with God.

Psalm 84:11 *For the Lord God is a Sun and Shield; the Lord bestows [present] grace* and *favor and [future] glory (honor, splendor, and heavenly bliss)! No good thing will He withhold from those who walk uprightly.*

4.   Be a tither

Malachi 3:10-12 *Bring all the tithes (the whole tenth of your income) into the storehouse, that there may be food in My house, and prove Me now by it, says the Lord of hosts, if I will not open the windows of heaven for you and our you out a blessing, that there shall not be room enough to receive it.*

And I will rebuke the devourer[insects and plagues] for your sakes and he shall not destroy the fruits of your ground, neither shall your vine drop its fruit before the time in the field, says the Lord of hosts. And all nations shall call you happy and blessed, for you shall be a land of delight, says the Lord of hosts.

5. Stay far from the workers of iniquity

(Backbiters, gossipers, ungodly people, and such)

Psalm 1:1-3 *Blessed (happy, fortunate, prosperous, and enviable) is the man who walks* and *lives not in the counsel of the ungodly [following their advice, their plans and purposes], nor stands [submissive and inactive] in the path where sinners walk, nor sits down [to relax and rest] where the scornful [and mockers] gather.*
But his delight and *desire are in the law of the Lord, and on His law (the precepts, the instructions, the teachings of God) he habitually meditates (ponders and studies) by day and by night.*
And he shall be like a tree firmly planted [and tended] by the streams of water, ready to bring forth its fruit in its season; its leaf also shall not fade or wither; and everything he does shall prosper[and come to maturity].

6. **Be a giver** indeed

Give to the poor, to the less privileged, give to your biological and spiritual parents.

Luke 6:38 *Give, and [gifts] will be given to you; good measure, pressed down, shaken together, and running over, will they pour into [the pouch formed by] the bosom [of your robe and used as a bag]. For with the measure you deal out [with the measure you use when you confer benefits on others], it will be measured back to you.*

7. **Spend time in prayer and in the Word daily**

Ephesians 6:10-18 *In conclusion, be strong in the Lord [be empowered through your union with Him];draw your strength in Him [that strength which His boundless might provides].*
Put on God's whole armor [the armor of a heavy-armed soldier which God supplies], that you may be able successfully to stand up against [all] the strategies and the deceits of the devil.
For we are not wrestling with flesh and blood [contending only with physical opponents], but against the despotisms, against the powers, against [the master spirits who are] the world rulers of this present darkness, against the spirit forces of wickedness in the heavenly (supernatural) sphere.

Therefore put on God's complete armor, that you may be able to resist and stand your ground on the evil day [of danger], and, having done all [the crisis demands], to stand [firmly in your place].

Stand therefore [hold your ground], having tightened the belt of truth around your loins and having put on the breastplate of integrity and of moral rectitude and right standing with God,

And having shod your feet in preparation [to face the enemy with the firm-footed stability, the promptness, and the readiness produced by good new, with all [manner of] prayer and entreaty. To that end keep alert and watch with strong purpose and perseverance, interceding in behalf s] of the Gospel of peace.

Lift up over all the [covering] shield of saving faith, upon which you can quench all the flaming missiles of the wicked [one].

And take the helmet of salvation and the sword that the Spirit wields, which is the Word of God.

Pray at all times (on every occasion, in every season) in the Spirit, with all [manner of] prayer and entreaty. To that end keep alert and watch with strong purpose and perseverance, interceding in behalf of all the saints (God's consecrated people).

8. Finally, **don't forsake fellowship with the brethren**.

Always be in church so that you can be in touch.

Hebrews 12:22-26 *But rather, you have come to Mount Zion, even to the city of the living God, the heavenly Jerusalem, and to countless multitudes of angels in festal gathering.*

And to the church (assembly) of the Firstborn who are registered [as citizens] in heaven, and to the God Who is Judge of all, and to the spirits of the righteous (the redeemed in heaven) who have been made perfect.

And to Jesus, the Mediator(Go-between Agent) of a new covenant, and to the sprinkled blood which speaks [of mercy], a better and *nobler* and *more gracious message than the blood of Abel [which cried out for vengeance].*

So see to it that you do not reject Him or *refuse to listen to* and *heed Him Who is speaking [to you now]. For if they [they Israelites] did not escape when they refused to listen* and *heed Him Who warned* and *divinely instructed them [here] on earth [revealing with heavenly warnings His will], how much less shall we escape if we reject* and *turn our backs on Him Who cautions* and *admonishes [us] from heaven?*

Then [at Mount Sinai]His voice shook the earth, but now He has given a promise: Yet once more I will shake and *make tremble not only the earth but also the [starry] heavens.*

If you desire to give your life to Jesus Christ or re-dedicate your life, I would be happy to lead you in a prayer of salvation.

Say after me:

"Lord Jesus Christ, I acknowledge You as my Lord and my personal Savior.

I surrender my life to you; take it and use it for your glory.

From today onward I am now one of your children, enjoying Your favor.

Cleanse me from my sins and renew me by Your blood.

Thank You Lord Jesus.

Amen"

Miracle of Beautiful Things

99

Miracle of Beautiful Things (Drop Lights)

Miracle Renovations (Island Countertop)

Another Miracle Reno

Miracle Renovations

(Bathroom Countertops & Sinks)

Miracle Clutch

Miracle Car Loan Payoff